SOME NOTES ON THE PHILOSOPHICAL BASIS OF HINDU EROTIC SCULPTURE

Kama Kala

SOME NOTES ON THE PHILOSOPHICAL BASIS OF HINDU EROTIC SCULPTURE

BY MULK RÂJ ANAND

NAGEL PUBLISHERS
GENEVA—PARIS—HAMBURG—NEW YORK

FOR W.G. ARCHER AND M.S. RANDHAWA

PREFACE

Some time ago a pioneer American critic of Indian art wrote, deploring the fact that while many of the sculptures of Konarak were masterpieces, they could not, for obvious reasons, be published to the world. This apologetic utterance may have been forced by a tradition which has passed, in Europe and America, from the period of ungoverned greed to the period of good intentions.

Dr. Alex Comfort has brilliantly described this phenomenon: "The terroristic god of Victorianism is gone, but he has left his footprints in the minds of a whole generation of parents and the obsessional traits of their children. . . Ritualistic cleanliness has replaced the older squalor!"

The outer concern for health and discipline, according to most enlightened medical opinion, generally betokens an insecurity of the inner life, expressed in psychosomatic disorder, obsessional and depressive patterns, in love inadequacy and delinquency.

This delinquency, whether it may be of the minor forms, recognised by the law, or the more dangerous types, which lead to aggression through the desire for domination over others, is essentially a sign of prematurity or of the survival of barbarism.

If the "mad hatter's tea party", which constitutes our present world society, is sadistic at every step, both overtly and covertly, it is because masochism becomes the main attribute of citizenship under barbarism. A code of morals drawn up by, and for, nomadic tribes, in a patriarchal society, has received accretions from Christian and other monastical orders and exercises vigilant control on our lives, ready to detect and punish, through the policeman, normal human impulses, even when the primitive codes have ceased to find acceptance or belief among enlightened men.

The name of such a society is death, not life! Its symbols are the concentration camp, the conscript and the hydrogen bomb.

Now in the agrarian and pastoral forms of Indian civilisation and culture, love, in all its spiritual and sexual connotations, was frankly accepted and clothed in the beautiful imagery of exalted poetry, in words, colours and stones. The life-principle was worshipped through the subtle doctrines of the Hindu Kaula *(noble) cult as well as through magical beliefs, rituals and practices, intended to release the unconscious through the play function of sex.*

The "One" supreme God, Brahman, had according to legend split himself into the "many", through desire. And the "many" sought to become "one" through the same desire.

The union of male and female thus became the symbol, from the earliest times, for the union of all forces, and the pleasure of the body in mating became, under accepted religious and social forms, linked with the sanctity of procreation and an end in itself. The concept of original sin and sexual secretiveness never formed any part of the intense phases of Indian culture.

There were, undoubtedly, bad periods of regression and suicidal fury, when patriarchal puritanism sought to control society. Also, certain decadent forms flourished in periods of regression.

But, by and large, the dominant impression which Hindu and Buddhist civilisations give us is of a tender humanism, in touch with the natural forces of impulse and idea, and aware of all those sensibilities which go to make the full, rich life of man into the poetry of existence rather than the nervous pose of endemic anxiety.

Thus it was that, in Indian plastic art, the human form became the expression of the sculptor's vision of the life force. The abstract values of religion were always realised in the concrete imagery of the human body, exaggerated and dramatised to the supernatural proportions of gods and goddesses, but instinct with the sap of life. And, in the imagery of the yakshas, nymphs, fauns, dryads, celestial dancers, demi-gods and urges, the inner tensions of nature are rendered with conviction and mastery.

In such an atmosphere, it is not surprising that the Maithuna (loving) couples abound, from the earliest cave temples through the mediaeval period down till the 18th century, as the very consecration of the drama of sex, energy flowing in myriads of forms. And, almost always, they are carved without any suggestion of pornography, but with the utmost tenderness and sensuous beauty.

Until recently some of the European critics have, for one reason or another, denied the essential values of Indian sculpture. For instance, the late Mr. Roger Fry said in his Last Lectures: *"Hindu art is singular in thus combining an extraordinary control of free plastic movement with a marked indifference to the structural mechanism. The Hindu artist's imagination is so enthralled by his feeling for the undulating and yielding movements of the body as a whole, and his feeling for the surface quality of the flesh replaces all his emphasis on these aspects, to the exclusion of that fundamental structure which occupied the other great schools of plastic design."*

As my friend Mr. Rudy von Leyden has suggested: "This statement mistakes the effect for the cause. Indian plastic art has an extraordinary capacity to imagine the surging forces of life in the inanimate matter of rock. The expanding forces are held, so to speak, by the surface that gives and contains like the skin of a fruit or even the skin of human flesh. There is no special preoccupation with the surface quality of flesh (as a matter of fact, the ancient sculptor may have ignored that quality by plastering and painting the surface) but rather a preoccupation with the essence of life which determines the surface and its swelling contour."

Similarly, the objections of critics like Fry to the Maithuna sculptures as introducing "irrelevant" interest into carving to distract the attention from the purpose of a work of art, cannot any longer be sustained. For many of the younger critics of Indian art in Europe themselves reject the desiccating effects of the previous generations of puritanism.

It is with a view to presenting the actual data of human form in Indian sculpture, particularly of the kind which has so far evoked the wrath of puritans, that I have put forward the beautiful plates of four talented photographers, Raymond Burnier, Sunil Janah, Moti Ram Jain and D.H. Sahiar. The photoprints will by themselves, I hope, reproduce the plastic qualities, inherent in this kind of sculpture, in bold relief. But I have added a tentative exposition of the philosophical and religious basis of Hindu erotic art, which may explain the inner basis of this art.

I have been encouraged by many friends to put out this essay and I wish to record my appreciation of their generous criticism. I must mention the help I have received from Dr. Hermann Goetz, Dr. Stella Kramrish and Mr. George Keyt in my various studies. My publisher, Dr. Louis Nagel, showed immense patience in the production of the book. And the two friends, who have been my companions in recent wanderings among books and physical sites, will find my gratitude acknowledged in the dedication.

M.R.A.

I

OF THE PRIMARY PASSIONS OF MANKIND, HUNGER AND LOVE, THE SMUG
and comfortable middle classes of the Victorian era turned away from the latter even more than
from the former. For the awakening of the people to the horrors and iniquities of the first
rapacious phase of the industrial revolution in England, as well as the undercurrents of the
revolt in the colonies and possessions of the British Empire, had forced the dominant sections
to concede to the poor and the disinherited a certain amount of social reform. But the prejudice against love, particularly in its sexual form, was more deeply rooted in Christian puritanism, being based on the doctrine of Original Sin: and while many of the romantic intelligentsia protested violently, in verse and prose, against hypocrisy and called for the frank acceptance
of sex and a return to the more wholesome pagan outlook of an earlier ''Merrie England'', the
cohorts of prudery did not begin to disperse against the attack of the rebels until the researches
of the anthropologists, Morgan, Fraser and Tylor, and the sexologists, Van der Velde, Bloch
and Havelock Ellis, began to reveal the existence of other fairly harmonious civilisations among
the so called ''savage'' peoples of the East. The barbarities perpetrated by the opposing forces in
the first world war further stimulated the more sensitive among the intellectuals to questionings

7

and quite a few of them began to seek honesty and vitality in the arts of the relatively unspoiled "dark" peoples with their "darker" gods. And the creative writers and popularisers of the twenties finally shocked the hypocrites into facing "the facts of life" and the tenderness of sex as the basis of human relations.

Meanwhile, whatever the implications of the ding–dong battle between "puritans" and "romantics" in the home country, the damage had been done in the suburbs of the Empire.

Says the Italian anthropologist, Paola Mantegazza: "Our Western civilisation approaches woman like an animal in heat, with hardly more than an animal comprehension of anatomy and human refinements. And yet the West has, up to very recently, considered its ignorant approach as superior! The tragic consequences of this ignorance are now being realised..."

For the Christian missionaries, who came with the proverbial Bible in hand to "civilise the heathen", had already led up to the attack against the "obscene", "native" cultures, and succeeded, to some extent, in corroding the basic beliefs of the indigenous religions, which had survived from the past, often merely as uninspired ritualistic pujapath, devoid of intellectual content. And the foreign rulers, recruited mostly from among the puritanical middle classes, brought their own ignorant and arrogant complacency about Western Christian civilisation to bear on the ways of life of the people they ruled, barring a few forward and courageous spirits who tried to get to know the heathen. And their collaborators from among the "natives", frequently educated in the colonial schools and colleges, as well as on probation in the universities "at home", became thoroughly anglicised, adopting the alien pruderies as the hallmark of culture, thus remaining ignorant of the heritage of their own lands. And a century of Europeanisation created, as Lord Macaulay had wished, an educated middle class, in our country, to whom Greece and Rome were more important than Magadha and Mahavalipuram. And generations of our people, among them the most intelligent, have been affected by the "grey disease", until the *obiter dicta* of most educated Indians about the carvings in Khajuraho or the Sun Temple at Konarak is not very different from that of the most obtuse of the erstwhile rulers. In fact, while some of the most valiant British archaeologists struggled hard to preserve the ancient monuments, their Indian successors have remained completely apathetic, and willingly lend their ears to any die-hards who declare their wish to replace the temples of Khajuraho, Konarak, Puri and Bhuvaneshwar with new modern temples! And while the younger intelligentsia of the West turns in admiration to our monuments, the false shame of our new bourgeois parades itself in the most abject apologies about the decadence of our mediaeval art, and prohibits even husbands and wives to hold hands on the sea-shore or to kiss in a public place. To be sure, the mental imperialism of the West seems to have succeeded in corrupting and perverting the outlook of the conquered more than the physical empire, now luckily overthrown.

It is necessary, therefore, to restate the fundamental postulates behind Hindu erotic art, so that the sexual principles which inform some of the most vital sculptures of Bhuvaneshwar, Konarak and Puri are made explicit, and the return is made towards an internal criticism, in terms of the intentions of the builders, rather than in terms of biased westerners, whether they are Christian missionaries or their conscious and unconscious disciples among the fanatical puritans in our own midst.

There are obvious difficulties of documentation in the way of Indian art, which handicap the understanding of almost every special aspect of it. So what is offered here are only some stray notes and tentative suggestions, which may be valuable if only because they may help to dispel the furtiveness which characterises all talk of Indian erotic art and to lift the taboos on the exhibition of art work expressing the theme of sex, frankly and in the full sunlight of understanding of something which lies at "the roots of life".

II

THE EROTIC SCULPTURE IN THE MEDIAEVAL TEMPLES DID NOT SPRING up suddenly through the perversity of some local Raja who wished to titillate his personal appetites by the contemplation of several permutations and combinations of the human body. As everyone knows, who has even the vaguest acquaintance with the metaphysical principles of Indian civilisation, the polarity of the male and female has been shown in much of our creative art.

According to Sjt. S.C. Dey of the Bhuvaneshwar archaeological department, the earliest instance of an amorous couple is to be found in a Jain pillar in the Lucknow Museum. It is not quite certain whether this anticipates the carvings of amorous couples in Bodh Gaya, Taxila, Mathura and Karla, but the extant remains are certainly part of a continouus tradition for the representation of couples in sexual poses, which began with the beginning of the sculpture in India and continued until the British put a legal ban on secular "obscene" art. When the Maurya, Gandhara, Kushan and Cupta traditions travelled down into the Deccan on the west and south, and to the Bay of Bengal in the east, before the first century of the Christian era, the Maithuna embrace appears and re-appears. And in the mediaeval revival it is resuscitated with even greater vigour from Ellora to Khajuraho downwards to Bhuvaneshwar, Konarak and Puri and the south Indian Saivaite temples, as well as Belur and Halebeid. The whole of Indian folk art is replete with sexual motifs and, from the metal and wood images of Bengal to the wood carvings on the ceremonial Rathas, or carriages for gods, attached to each temple, there is the most intricate and tender embellishment of the theme of human love perhaps in all world art. Undoubtedly, however, the sexual carvings and reliefs in the temples of Khajuraho, Bhuvaneshwar, Konarak and Puri have invited greater attention from the prudes because of the greater profusion of the Maithuna couples and the boldness and elemental honesty of the sculpture, as well as the formal qualities of the carvings. No one who comes face to face with the magnificent sculpture in Khajuraho and Konarak can turn away, from sheer obsessional prejudice, but feels compelled to linger and appreciate the skill of the carver attempting the seemingly most impossible postures, not only frontally, but in the corners

10

and niches of the temples where it would be difficult to work in the ordinary way. And if, as in Khajuraho, there become visible, within the precincts of a group of temples, creative architecture and sculpture enough to compare with the products of the whole European Renaissance, the awe-struck visitor is merely dumb and aghast in the vain attempt to understand how such a miraculous achievement was at all possible!

What, then, were the ideals of the builders of the ancient and mediaeval temples? How did they live? And what were the emotions and passions which moved them in those remote times?

III

ADMITTEDLY, WE INDIANS HAVE DISPLAYED A VERY poor sense of history, and there are few contemporary records which might reproduce for us the atmosphere of those bygone ages. And yet to the extent to which the past has been uncovered, through the translations of Sanskrit and Pali texts, certain hints and references have become available, which suggest that the eras of the earliest creative arts in India, though stamped with the genius of man, as is, indeed, all history, were entirely different in their temper from the present day complex industrialised age.

In those days, there was a certain high condition, built on the fabric of a rural, agrarian society, where men's mouths uttered hymns and incantations and poetical proverbs in the face of nature's beneficent or dread potencies, even as we now speak in prose. As the earliest known invaders, the Aryans, came down into the Indus and Gangetic plains, they evolved a pantheon on the basis of their response to nature. The fire which had always been the mainstay of their nomadic life was exalted to the stations of the god Agni; the terrible storms that raged among the dense dark forests, and in the mountains, were symbolised as the god Rudra; the benevolence of nature was worshipped as Brahma. And as they began to occupy the most fecund wheatlands by subduing the original neolithic inhabitants of the country, the Dravidians, they were affected by the earth gods, the spiritual fervours and the magical rites of the indigenous tribes. There were *Yakshas* and *Yakshis*, tree spirits, among the conquered people; there were *Nagas* and *Naginis*, snake spirits; there were fauns and dryads and nymphs and fairies. For in the fabulous eyelids of the Dravidian peoples everything had a soul. And this soul was in the process of transmigration from one incarnation to another, according to the law of *Karma*, through which good deeds and bad deeds assured a higher or lower rebirth until the attainment of *Moksha*, release. Although the subjugated societies were characterised as snub nosed Dasyus by the Aryans and were later reduced to a lower status in the fourfold hierarchy of caste, imposed by the dominant groups, the invaders adopted almost all the native beliefs, took wives from among them, since they themselves had brought few women, and a great synthesis began of the two stocks which resulted in the elaboration of a more complex pantheon of myths, fables, wise sayings and geometric designs about space, time and the interactions of the stars in their courses.

Already, fifteen centuries before Christ, in the *Rig Veda*, the Aryans had sung tenderly about the relations between man and woman. And the following poem suggests a very sensitive and lyrical conception of human desire among the opposite sexes, springing from an intense realisation of love and the beauty and exalted dignity of woman.

I am a poet, Dad's a leech,
and mother grinds corn on the quern;
as cows go following, one on one,
we all seek wealth in different ways.

The horse likes a light-laden cart,
gay hosts attract the laugh and jest;
man longs for woman, natural as
the parched frogs longing for the rains.

And, apart from the vaulting ambitions of the philosopher to reach the limits of metaphysical speculation, the *Hymn of Creation* states the creative principle in a manner which was to supply the foundation for all fundamental restatements of the origin of the universe and human life.

Desire, then, at first arose within it,
Desire, which was the earliest seed of spirit.
The bond of Being, in Non-Being sages,
Discovered searchings in their hearths with wisdom.

In the light of the vague doctrine of desire as the cause of the world, the philosophy of *Kama*, wish, desire, carnal gratification, lust, love and affection, was growing up in the Vedic period, through the activities of popular priest-craft and Dravidian practice. The charms of love are frequently mentioned in the *Atharva Veda*, the last of the four holy books, probably sung almost contemporaneously with the earlier *Vedas*, the *Rig*, *Sama* and *Yajur*, but classified later. The philosophical attitude is a simple one, recommending love-life, or family life, as the necessary condition of humanity at a certain stage. A harmonious family is that in which both the husband and wife are happy and dedicated to the procreation of numerous children, preferably sons and more sons, for sons are indispensable to the maintenance of an unbroken line, for the performance of the funeral rites over the father's dead body, and for

the worship of the spirits of dead ancestors. There are nearly forty poems among the five hundred and thirty six hymns, prayers, incantations and charms in the *Atharva Veda* (Trans. C.R. Lanman, Harvard Oriental Series, Vol. VII, and VIII, Cambridge, Mass. 1905) devoted to the subject of *Kama*. Let us mention them here to give some idea of the scope of the interest evinced in human relations in the Vedic period.

"For successful child-birth (II). Imprecation of spinsterhood on a woman (14). A love spell, with a sweet herb (34). To secure a woman's love (72). To get a husband for a woman (81). Against a rival wife, with a plant (117). For fecundity (127). To command a woman's love (130). For recovery of virility, with a plant (149). The incantation of the lover entering the girl's house by night; to put the household to sleep (151). For successful conception (265). Two charms, to win a woman's love (287). For birth of sons (288). Against premature birth (293). Against jealousy (293). For winning a spouse (325). For matrimonial happiness (339). For successful pregnancy, with an armlet (341). To obtain a wife (342). To win affection (347). For virile power (354). To win a woman (355). Two charms to win a woman's love (380). For pregnancy (401). Against a rival woman (411). Husband and wife to one another (411). The wife to the husband (412). To win and fix a man's love, with a plant (412). To cure jealousy (416). To destroy one's virile power (465). Against a woman rival, with a plant (467). To guard a pregnant woman from demons (493). To Kama (521). Magic stanzas for marriage ceremonies (704-753). Of and to Desire (985)."

From this compilation it would seem that husbands and wives had their difficulties pretty much as we have these tensions now; and the remedies offered in the *Atharva Veda* are not unlike those which have been offered in all ages; only then the consultant on marital affairs was the priest or the quack; and now we have the psychoanalyst and the family doctor.

The surprising thing is the awareness, so early, of the whole problem of man-woman relationship, and its recognition as a fact of life as against the beating about the gooseberry bush of our Europeanised age. And, apart from the herbs, plants, philtres and amulets, the dictums laid down about suggestion and persuasion, the elementary eugenics, as well as the emotional and mental hygiene of attunement, all couched as magic no doubt, offer a tremendous advance on such concepts amongst other contemporaneous civilisations.

And the whole subject is treated as a profound concept in the sense of the holy mystery of life, which sets the tone for all subsequent literature on the subject.

In the sixth part of the *Chandogya Upanishad*, the Brahmin Svetaketu, one of the first redactors of literature on sex, is spoken of as receiving the key to all knowledge in the form of the *Vedic Maha-Vakya*, "great formula" *Tat Tvam Asi*, "That art thou". This Brahmin was a master of sacred love and brought the highest sanctions to bear on the art of love.

IV

DURING THE THOUSAND YEARS OR SO OF THE ARYAN AND DRAVIDIAN synthesis, a rich intricate fabric of social relations was being built up as substratum of life on the lush lands of the fertile plains of Bharat. The little village "republics" were the units of this cellular organisation, autonomous and self absorbed in husbandry, in which none owned land, but everyone had certain rights in it, to till it or to live on the tiller in return for certain services, like the potter, the weaver, the locksmith, the school teacher, etc. Even the local Raja or the Maharaja in the capital did not own land as private property but had the right to collect revenue in kind from the peasantry in lieu of the protection he offered against invaders with his soldiery, or for keeping dikes, dams, canals and tracks in good repair, for the bullock carts and the horse chariots to move on.

In the personal histories, or the novels, of that time, the two epics, the *Ramayana* and the *Mahabharata*, which narrate the legendary story of the Aryan conquest of India, we have glimpses of the human conflicts of that age and we see the evolution of the confused moral laws of this early civilisation. These were more clearly laid down later in an appendix to the epic *Mahabharata*, the *Bhagavad Gita*. The beauty and devotion of woman is the dominating theme of these humanistic narratives. Draupadi, Damayanti, Savitri, Sita and a host of other females emerge as highly individualised characters though tending to become symbolic. The daily life of these women, their toilet, their blandishments, their emotional urges, all are narrated in intricate detail and with such charm as to indicate the existence of a uniquely sensitive civilisation. Although the metaphysical postulates of the *Vedas* and *Upanishads* conduce towards a certain formalism about marriage, exalting it into a sense of duty to the race, in actual fact the free marriage called the *Gandharva* was often practised, especially by kings and sages.

The *Gandharva* morality continued right into the mediaeval period, because of the sanctions given to it by the poets of the classical renaissance. For instance, Kalidas glorified the tale of Sakuntala, taken from the *Mahabharata*, in which the hero, King Dushyantha, marries the heroine, Sakuntala, in the hermitage of her foster father, according to the *Gandharva* rite. This rite entailed a declaration by the man to the woman, or the woman to the man, "I love you", and they forthwith accepted each other in marriage and exercised their conjugal rights. There was no priest or witness of the union and no gods were invoked. In fact, Bharata, from whom India takes its name, was born of the Gandharva marriage of Dushyantha and Sakuntala.

14

It is likely that pagan practices were common among the lower castes, who had retained the fantasies of the Dravidian civilisation against the patriarchical concepts of the Aryans. And in so far as the culture of the suppressed people appealed to the Kshatriya Kings and sages, they seem to have accepted *Gandharva* rites more easily than the Brahamanical order.

So the customs of the body politic, which emerge from these epics, also reveal the shadows. For side by side with the subtle doctrines resulting from pure feats of the intellect and the penetrating imaginative analysis of the emotions, there emerges a certain low condition to which the men of the sub castes are being reduced, feeding on the roots and harbouring deep resentments against the upper caste orders.

But the chief impression is of a series of qualitatively profound philosophies of existence embodied in the aphorisms and proverbs of sages, who lived in retirement in caves and forest groves, and whose thoughts later came to be collected in the so called forest books, the *Brahmanas* and the *Upanishads*.

The essence of these speculations was the inauguration of a supra-sensual kingdom of belief in the One Absolute God, *Brahman*, who splits himself through desire into the *Many* and into whom the Unit, or One God, all multiple elements wish to return.

There is no doubt that this central doctrine, which has emerged from the Vedic and Dravidian synthesis and from the forest books, has held sway over the whole of subsequent Indian thought by its prodigious plausibility, its exalted conception of a Supreme Deity, who has the highest attributes, is completely incomprehensible to the human intellect, is attainable only through mystical intuition and is yet a prototype of the Father, the embodiment of all that is in this universe, the being and the becoming, the unity of all life, the ultimate symbol of creation. The rational mind cannot really describe him, and man can only say "It is not this—not that". And yet the parallelism of human impulse to procreate offers a clue to His creation of the cosmos:

"He desired
I am One
Let me be many that creation may be."

The parable of human desire for progeny is pressed further. The Supreme Being impregnates nature through His longing for the opposite: and the pull or attraction between the two principles becomes the source of all life. The spirit *(Atman)* "alone is the aspect of person" *(Purusa)*. This person in the beginning "was of such sort as are a man and a woman closely embraced. He desired a second. He caused that spiritual self of his to fall atwain. Thence came into being husband and wife... He had intercourse with her. Thence were human beings engendered". In the same way he and she assuming other human forms begot their like in these animal types.

Says Krishna, the incarnation of the supreme deity in the *Bhagavad Gita:*

"I am the Lust that procreates."   16

Again:

"The matrix of all forms, born from all wombs in Nature, Prakriti. I, the father, giver of seed."

The male and female forms thus become the manifestation of duality, desired by the Supreme God, the earthly symbols of manyness and procreation:

"The Yoni and the Lingam symbolise the creation of the world. Their union represents Karma (action)!"

VATULA SHUDDHA AGMA

And just as our human love is seen as a symbol of the great love of the Supreme God, so the Joy of physical union reflects the limitless Joy of the Deity in creation:

"In the embrace of his beloved a man forgets the whole world—everything both within and without; in the very same way, he who embraces the self knows neither within nor without."

BRIHADARANYAKA UPANISHAD

Naming each thing and fixing each symbol is but the most inadequate way of expressing the nature of the functions of the Supreme God.

For He who enjoys greatest joy, or is Anand, Bliss Incarnate, is beyond reach, except to the most selfless seeker.

As against His Joy, the condition of human existence is merely a lack of Joy, a form of suffering, which will last as long as men and women do not struggle to emancipate themselves from birth and rebirth, through worship and dedication and merge with the Supreme God or Bliss. Our human happiness gives but a glimpse of the boundless Joy in store for us, in so far as we recognise our true self for the briefest moment. For this reason, the sacred act of procreation is to be valued, as it affords the intensest moments of Joy we can experience while we strive for the ultimate and complete absorption into the Deity.

With that characteristic genius for elaborating the highest sanctions, the ancient Hindus, therefore, accepted an anthropomorphic view of God, in which not only is human sexual pleasure exalted as the Joy nearest to the realisation of God, but everything in life becomes divine, every action becomes, when properly understood, the concrete expression of some universal law, the shimmering surface of the deeper connection, the image of a less or more intimate approach to the Supreme Bliss, the starting point for the attempt to pierce the dreamy veil to the shadows which are more consecrated, and beyond whose dazzle of muslin lies the superabundant Joy...

18

Certainly, the odour and sweat of sex is made sacred, and no shame attaches to it:

> "The woman is the fire, her womb the fuel, the invitation of a man the smoke. The door is the flame, the entering the ember, pleasure the spark. In this fire the gods form the offering. From this offering springs forth the child."
>
> (CHANDOGYA UPANISHAD—5,8, 1-2)

The mystic syllable AUM becomes the symbolic equivalent of the erotic image:

> "The union of the sexes is equivalent to the mystic syllabe AUM. When the two sexes come together, each fulfils the desire of the other."

As the highest tide of Upanishadic thought reached out to ideals which defied human understanding, there was much elaboration of ritual to afford access by the laity to the secret and difficult knowledge of the holy teachings.

The Vedas had conceded: "Ideas to the learned: Wood and stones to the ignorant." And it is likely that a highly intricate psychology of ritualistic worship was evolved by the Brahmins for knitting together the Hindu caste order. And many of the elementary sacrifices performed in Vedic times over the sacred fire, including the joining of man and woman in a marriage, acquired deeper significance through the forest books. And torches were lit, and the bells tolled in the great halls of worship at the *arti* hour when hands were joined before the idols, in the vicinity of every village, and the priests exacted their dues for officiating at these ceremonies. And perhaps the poor, exploited, low caste men spoke in lowered tones outside the shrine, for they were increasingly denied entry into the house of God and were outside the orbit of *Dharma*, religion; *Karma*, destiny; *Artha*, works; and *Moksha*, release.

V

UPON THIS SCENE ENTERED A MAN OF SENSIBILITY, GAUTAMA THE Buddha.

He was struck by the jugglery of the Hindu priestcraft with words and images as was Mahavira, the austere, naked Jina, his near contemporary. And he saw the outcasts rotting at the far end of the villages. And he held debates with the Brahmins and often confounded them in argument. And, unable to effect reforms, he hoisted the flag of revolt against the exalted religion of his forefathers.

The fundamental fact of the earthly universe is pain, he said. And there is no way to escape from this suffering, to which man is condemned by the cycle of birth and rebirth, except to shun false desire and to practise the fourfold path: right speech, right conduct, right thoughts, right deeds...

The ultimate state of release is not the realisation of God, but of Nirvana, the reservoir of bliss, from which there is no return to the earthly state, subject to the transmigration of soul through the performance of good or bad *Karma*...

And this dream of the pure clouds, above the acrid insinuations of men against each other because of their position in the Hindu caste order, inspired hundreds and thousands of people to follow the enlightened one, a high caste Kshatriya prince who had left home to seek the truth and preach it to all suffering humanity.

And a great Joy was set free in the country, the bells tolling in heaven at the release of men from the shackles of the most degenerate and greedy Brahmins. A new concept of holiness spread over the land:

"I call not a man a Brahmin, because he is born of a Brahmin mother, such an one, if affluent, may be addressed as 'Sir'. But he who is without worldly belongings and is free from attachment, him I call a Brahmin."

DHAMMAPADA, 14

The villages that flowed like abscesses into the town, heard the healing message. And, from the odorous men in the crowds of sick and old, and from the women who had begun to be suppressed by the priests, jealous of their power over men, arose the breath of a prayer which was purer than that heard for some time. And the populace sped to the monasteries established by the order of Bhikkus, monks, who had renounced the path of suffering and timidly knelt before the light of the Buddha which shone in their hearts. And not all the misery that came to them through the persecution of the Brahmins could blow out the lamp that Gautama had lit.

For a thousand years or more, the struggle between the men of the new gospel, of the undogmatic weak and the downtrodden, against the men of the established order, raged in all parts of India. The mightiest of Emperors, Ashoka, accepted the new faith and sent out missionaries to many lands to preach the new words of tenderness.

The inner conflict of ideas was, however, fraught with strange consequences; whereas the new pure teaching had rid the old faith of the Hindus of many of the putrid accretions, the morte subtle psychology of Hindu ritualistic worship penetrated Buddhism in time. And in a century or so after the death of Gautama the negative features of the Hinayana gospel had been humanised by the urges of the populace, with a mythology as replete with the graces of the imagination as had been the pantheon of the Hindus.

Speaking the words of the blessed one, and discoursing all over the land, the monks picked up the practice of *Yoga*, union, and set forth the doctrine, even as the small dark people of the land wanted it, conceding to magic, and the mental images of each area, the sanctity through which a complete alliance with life became possible.

Thus there came to be defined three created realms in Buddhist iconography through which beings pass to be reborn: *Kama-loka*, the world of desires; *Rupa-loka*, the world of pure forms, beyond desires; and *A-rupa-loka*, the world without forms. And the example of the Buddha was cited as that of the sage who broke the power of desire, even as he had routed the forces of death, in order to rise into the timeless infinite of *Nirvana*. Not for everyone was such a triumph possible. For face to face with the excruciating paradox of life, the more alive, the more difficult to bear, the laity were not prevented from devoting themselves to the pursuit of the bitter-sweet delusion.

VI

AND YET THE DISCIPLINE OF *YOGA* WAS BY THIS TIME ACCEPTED AS AN ideal both by the Hindus and the Buddhists. Yogic practice was designed to deepen the interior realisations, so that the extrovert experiences fall aside and the higher and more rarefied worlds of faculty and experience are attained. These latter are themselves divided into further strata, each inhabited by a distinct class of celestial beings.

According to the central principle of *Yoga*, there are distinct differences between different kinds of beings, due to the relative position of the subtle centres of the body. Thus each human or animal body is represented by a diagram, *Yantra*, formed by the main centres, and the proportions of *Yantra* determine the relative adjustments of the characteristics that go to make an individual. It is possible, by adopting certain definite postures, to change the relative position of the subtle centres and thus evolve a new *Yantra*. And if we can maintain this new relationship of forces in us for some time, the new balance will so affect our perceptions that we may come into touch with the kind of being represented in the new diagram.

The postures or *asanas* of *Yoga* are specifically designed to promote this end. And they are roughly of two kinds: the *padma-asana*, or the lotus seat, the posture of attainment, and the various erotic postures. Of both these there are eighty four in number, and they are frequently represented in pictorial literature.

The teaching of the *Yoga Sutras* was designed to get rid of the hindrances of *Klesa*, the pain of the world caused by *Avidya*, ignorance, *Asmita*, the crude ego, *Raja*, attachment: *Dvesa*, hatred, *Abhinivesa*, clinging to life. For the inherent perfection of the essential personality was an ideal which had percolated among the ordinary people as the highest value, short of the achievement of *Kaivalya*, the perfect isolation, final emancipation, exclusiveness and detachment.

VII

DURING THE CENTURIES FOLLOWING THE ACCEPTANCE OF PARALLEL doctrines of the Hindus and the Buddhists, there were many accretions, springing from popular beliefs and superstitions. And yet the ideal of *Moksha*, or release, was pursued in common with a tolerance for the efforts of the least of men, as Krishna had said in the *Bhagavad Gita*.

All the same, in spite of the tremendous heterogeneity of outlook, the attainment by man, the microcosm, of *Brahman*, the macrocosm, the rise from the individual *atman* to the Self which is within, is supposed to secure the possession of Divine Cosmic Power, beyond anxiety strife and change. This came to be accepted by all and sundry as the real goal of life.

But because there is no aspect of existence, animate or inanimate, in which we can fail to perceive the Divine, the dynamism of the phenomenal world and the permanence of the animating principle can be experienced at one and the same time, as the identical mystery —the trancendent serene being, who is immanent, and yet partially manifest, in the phenomenal becoming of the universe.

The habitual preaching of generation after generation of learned men left a substratum of metaphysical awareness that informs even the mundane literature and art of what is called the Classical Renaissance in India, which coincided with the Gupta period about the fourth century. So complete is the hold of this transcendentalism that what was then called *Kala* (Art) is throughout reflective, at one remove or another, of this philosophy of the life process.

Thus in the series of Sanskrit plays during this age, as well as in the pictorial representation of mythology in the temple, the same vital principles and situations are dramatised, so that they carry hints about the immanent Gods, towards whom men reverently lift their heads,

24

even as they delight the senses and afford *Rasa,* delight, the aesthetic counterpart of *Ananda,* joy, which was the object of mystical union.

Undoubtedly, there is much individualist creative activity in the poetry and paintings of the Gupta Age, and in the rich, expansive feudal empire the world becomes a kind of kaleidoscope, which reveals the loveliest flowers in its turnings, and one finds wonder and delight in contemplating the hauntingly tender beauties. There are Bacchanalian scenes in Ajanta, and amorous scenes which appear to bring the ineffable luxury of bodies burning with passion before one's eyes, a pagan, sunny laughter of the dark sensuous bodies as though the painters were mocking at all mysteries beyond that of the moment. But even in this splendrous art, which exalts all human emotion and feelings, we are dimly aware of the evanescence of the phenomenal world. The lovely girls in the poems of Kalidas carry forever between their wine jar hips the secret of the sensual mystery, as also the purpose of the God for continuous creation through the profoundly holy and terrible, beautiful sexual act, the source of all life. The profuse erotic scenes which begin now to be seen in the temples are not only meant, therefore, to excite the onlooker but as intimations of the Divine in those very situations where we are most likely to forget them. Silently flows the sap of the creative life, and it is at one's peril that one can ignore it.

In the masterly text book of love, the *Kama Sutra,* the sage Vatsyayana, who was probably the contemporary of Kalidas, seeks to fit *Kama,* sex, into the four-fold Hindu scheme of life. "Man will attain perfect happiness by serving *Artha, Kama,* and *Dharma,* in this manner. Cultured men engage in activities that do not endanger one's prospects in the other world that do not entail loss of wealth and that are withal pleasant."

The four-fold scheme, to which Vatsyayana refers, had already come to be accepted as a rationalisation of ordinary practice. *Dharma,* the practice of socal righteousness, *Artha,* the pursuit of prosperity, *Kama,* the pursuit of pleasure, and *Moksha,* the striving after liberation, were all considered complementary as well as exclusive of each other. Thus *Dharma,* or righteousness, and *Moksha,* or liberation, go together as do *Artha,* or prosperity, and *Kama,* or pleasure. Also, symbolically, righteousness and prosperity, and liberation and pleasure, have features in common: the first pair binds while the second releases one from attachment. The virtuous and the prosperous man is steeped in worldly values, but the man who seeks release from the trammels of existence or wishes to drown himself in the pleasures of this world, tend to ignore both wealth and morality. The transition from the life of pleasure to the dedicated life of the saint has often been very sudden in India, while those who have chosen the good path in the world have also succeeded in amassing wealth. So the sanctions established by religion seemed to show deep insight into the practical issues involved. And, though sexual pleasure was considered the symbol of the Supreme Bliss, and even interpreted as one of the ways leading to it, the elasticity of the whole conception now gave room for indulgence in it as pleasure. It is conceivable that these concessional doctrines were emerging because of the large numbers of people who, while accepting the tenets of Hindu religion, were unable to live up to the seemingly pessimistic concept implied in existence as suffering and release and absorption into *Brahman* as the only goal. A rich, fashionable feudal aristocracy had arisen which had the means of enjoying the pleasures of the world, and women, who had been ascribed an ignominious position in the Hindu social system by the law giver, Manu, had regained some of the respect they had enjoyed in the Vedic Age. The liberal Buddhist attitude towards the outcasts was leading to a greater tolerance towards the lower orders from the Hindus as well.

Vatsyayana's encyclopaedia of sex is avowedly a compendium based on previous texts on the general and special problems of sex by Nandi, Svetaketu, son of Uddalaka, Vabhravya Panchala, Dattaka, Charnyans, Ghotamukha, Gonardiya, Gonikapatra, Suvarnanaha and Kuchumara. All these writers as well as the author of the *Kama Sutra* reflect the more or less scientific or psychological aspect of their enquiries, Vatsayayana deliberately treating his book as a part of the medical system of *Ayurveda*. The hypothesis seems to be that since sexual curiosity is, apart from the awakening of sensibility towards Reality, also one of the main causes of the perversion of the mind, it must be satisfactorily explained and analysed, so that such education can lead not only to healthy enjoyment of the variegated pleasures of the body but also clarify the mind of all filth attached to the secret act. Also, no hidden longings should remain in the mind of the seeker after *Moksha*, which might prove to be a hindrance to spiritual progress afterwards.

Truly, as Sir Richard Burton, the Orientalist and translator once wrote, "this work (the Kama Sutra), then, which has stood the test of centuries, has placed Vatsyayana among the immortals; on this, and on him, no better elegy or eulogy can be written than the following lines:

'So long as lips shall kiss, and eyes shall see,
So long lives this, and This gives life to Thee.' "

One might go further and say that the whole of subsequent Indian art tradition will remain incomprehensible and, at the best, be appreciated only from partial viewpoints, if the connoisseur has not previously read this classic scientific text. Certainly, there can be no understanding of the erotic sculpture of Indian temples without reference to the postures descibed by Vatsyayana and the attitude of educated people towards these sculptures will remain that of the chelas of the missionary mediocrities of Europe.

"After having finished his education, the accomplished man", says Vatsyayana at the beginning of his discourse, "should set himself to acquiring wealth, and having earned it, or come into it by succession, should lead the life of a man of fashion". The hero is supposed to be well-versed in the literary arts, able to take part in competitions of poetic skill, a man of good taste, who knows all about the architecture of a house, can lay out a garden, choose paintings and sculptures, appreciate the arts of music and dance, clothes, jewellery and perfumes.

The woman, especially the courtesan, has to learn the sixty-four arts from early childhood, this education emphatically including music, dance, aesthetic of the plastic and literary arts, as well as of jewellery, decoration and flower arrangement.

The whole of Vatsyayana's system hinges on the psychology of erotic education informed by the highest delicacy and sensitiveness. For instance, in the chapter "The art of winning the confidence of the wife", "the approach to the newly married wife" is analysed, "need of

26

gentle methods" stressed, "necessity of winning the girl's love before marital relations" enjoined, and the technique of approach is explained from "the embrace" to "the next step, the kiss", "the third step, intimate talk", "stimulation of the mammilla" and the "technique of manipulation".

The chapter "Classification of Sexual Unions" includes instruction on the following subjects: "The two aspects of sexual union, classification according to dimensions of genital organs, kinds of union according to size, kinds of union according to character of passion, kinds of union according to duration, kinds of union, four categories of sexual gratification."

The chapter "Art of Embraces" includes: "Sixty four accessories of sexual intercourse, the technique of embrace, intimate embraces, embraces during the act of coitus, rubbing or squeezing as a pleasant accessory process."

The chapter "Art and Technique of Kissing" includes: "The order of the kiss and other forms of love-play, the technique of the kiss, three kinds of the lip kiss for women, love-play with kissing by wager, the concurrent or responsive kiss, kisses on other parts of the body, other forms of special kisses, kissing of the hands and feet."

The chapter "Attitudes in sexual communion" includes: "Three attitudes in tight-fit unions, four attitudes in loose-fit unions, other attitudes in sexual unions, front to back or reverse attitude, attitude of chase or quadrupedal attitudes, group coitus in matriarchal societies, coitus in and on woman condemned."

The chapter "Reversed normal attitude and technique of intromission" includes: "Two ways in which a woman can take the active role, how to enhance the pleasure in coitus of a woman, signs of increasing passion in a woman, ten ways of penial intromission, three manners in reversed normal attitudes."

The chapter "Conduct before and after sexual intercourse" includes: "How one should receive a desired woman, what should be done after coitus, how to increase passion of lovers, varieties of coitus according to nature of passion, what a lover should do in case of quarrel with the beloved."

These and other themes are treated in some of the Gupta works and in the whole of mediaeval temple sculpture, almost as though they were authentically drawn from life. Vatsyayana mentions the sexual habits and customs of different parts of India, such as those of Balhika (Bactria), Vidharba, Malva, Avanti, Maharashtra, Abhira, Saurashtra, Aparantha, Dakshinapatha, Vanasvasa, Kustala, etc. It is probable that he travelled to these places for his research, but it is certain that he lived either in the ancient city of Ujjain, which was the capital of Avanti, or very near Khajuraho, where the greatest profusion of erotic sculptures can be seen apart from Konarak. The sage does not mention Pataliputra or many regions east of Avanti, but he is likely to have known about the love life of the Ganges delta. And, at any rate, the cultural tradition of the Gupta empire spread through the length and breadth of India, and as the literary works were copied and taken to different seminaries, so the guilds of craftsmen moved often from temple to temple (even as labourers and skilled technicians move today from dam to dam) and the teaching of the arts and sciences accompanied the new schools of Brahmanical Theism, which arose on the foundations of Vedic religion in the early and late mediaeval periods.

VIII

THE FERMENT WHICH WAS WITNESSED IN THE GUPTA AGE HAD BEEN simmering from below the surface of Hindu society for nearly a thousand years. And the incredibly complex system of beliefs grouped together under the symbol *Aum* had acquired such a multiplicity of Gods that the pantheon was teeming, as, indeed, was the population of this prolific, lush continent in which many races, tribes and peoples had come to live on a more or less tolerant basis of co-existence. The seeming anarchy of religious beliefs and practices was held in check by the underlying unity of belief in the monistic Upanishadic doctrine of *Brahman*, the Supreme God, and a traditional way of life, though the fissiparous tendencies nearly destroyed it under the impact of Jainism and Buddhism. But, as always, under attack from all sides, Hindu society rallied and revived and regrouped its forces to extend its sway for another thousand years.

29

Apart from the *Darshanas,* or the various schools of thought which offered different interpretations about Reality, the doctrine of henotheism had begun to assert itself, according to which the most important Gods of the pantheon were being exalted to the supreme Godhood by large sects, all the other gods being reduced to the position of incarnations of this supreme deity.

This theistic assertion brought three chief deities to the fore: Vishnu, who was the incarnation of Brahma in his benevolent qualities; Siva, who symbolised the Supreme God, or creator, preserver and destroyer of the universe; Shakti, the consort of Siva, who was both mother and destroyer alternately. The faith known as Vaishnavism flourished mostly in northern and central India, while Saivaism held sway in the South and South East, as well as certain pockets in the northern hills, and Saktism was dominant in eastern India and in some part of the South West in Malabar.

It will be remembered that the Ultimate Reality, *Brahman,* was described in the Upanishad negatively as "Not this—not that" and was declared to be ineffable and *unknowable,* except through mystical intuition. The new schools of philosophy, in which the practical theistic faiths began to find their sanctions, affirmed that the Reality behind phenomena is *knowable.* It is, in fact, consciousness itself.

This Consciousness is the pure unity behind all *forms* of consciousness whether these be sensation, emotion, instinct, will or reason. But it assumed particularity through *Mava,* the reflection or mode of consciousness, or surface consciousness, which is in its seed the cosmic *Samskara* but empirically embraces the ordinary world.

In so far as the forms of surface consciousness were admitted and the way opened for the practical human mind, *Buddhi,* to operate, these new schools of thought conceded to mankind a way of life more consonant with its frailties. Thus the face behind the mask remained more or less the same *Brahman,* the invisible source of all things, pure and unchanging, the mysterious power in which all operations grow. But, reflecting this unity, there was the whole phenomenal universe in which everything was in the process of transformation or change through *Karma,* from plants to human kind.

Since the phenomenal world is Maya, all our lives are also expressions of this illusory stuff, and attachment to them leads to frustration and suffering. Only in turning away the mind from *Mava* to the Ultimate Reality is peace to be found.

But whereas in the past ages the way to union with the Supreme God lay through yoga, now it is conceded that through personal devotion or *bhakti,* where the worshipper regards himself as the creature and servant of Vishnu, Siva or Sakti, the deity in human form, man can seek *Moksha* or release.

The waves of Brahmanical theistic cults which swept over India gave a tremendous impetus to Hinduism, in so far as it gathered into its folds an even more intricate ritual in the hundreds of new temples which were built, giving the original rather pessimistic hypothesis all the glamour of music and dance and colour. A god who found immense popularity with the lay public was Krishna, originally a local cowherd prince of Mathura, who had figured as the helper of the five Pandava heroes of the *Mahabharata* epic, and who was now exalted to be the most familiar incarnation of Vishnu, the blessed one. The parable of his sports with his

30

consort, Radha, and the milkmaids, was made a symbol of the *lila*, sport of God with human beings whom He loves and with whom he continually plays hide-and-seek. And a whole literature and art grew up around the joyous dalliances of Krishna with Radha and the gopinis sanctifying the most human of urges and desires among the populace, with their love of pageants.

All the old harvest festivals of the ancient agrarian communities were strung together like a garland around the seasons of the year, and the heart of the populations beat to the rhythm of the drums and cymbals and bells in the temple, spiritualising each act of the profanest of the pariahs and knitting them into the fabric of a living Hindu society.

Thus it was that, in spite of the chaos produced by the successive invasions from the north west, Hinduism lasted out through the centuries. Albeit, it was on the defensive, and many corrupt practices crept into it, and it tended to weave pattern after pattern out of its rich variety of beliefs and interpretations, so that there is an air of ossification about the mediaeval codes and compendiums of the *Puranas*. At each difficult phase, however, it seemed to find powerful support from some revivalism or the other. And the succession of Hindu mediaeval mystic poets and saints from Shankara, Tulsidas, Ramanuja, Kabir, Tuka Ram and Mira Bai, some of whom wrote in the *prakrits*, people's speech, rather than in the difficult Sanskrit, kept the flame of resurgent Hinduism alive, burning with a searing quality, dazzling and fierce.

IX

ALL THROUGH THE MEDIAEVAL PERIOD, FURTHER DEVELOPMENTS WERE taking place in the attitude towards *Brahman*, besides that which made him knowable in and through the phenomenal world, or as *Maya* in contradistinction to *Brahman* the unknowable, Ultimate Reality of the Upanishads.

The three contendings religions, Hinduism, Buddhism and Jainism, had begun to absorb much ritual from each other in order to attract the dissident followers of their rivals and absorb them to themselves. About the 10th and 11th century, the Advaita and Vaishnava cults of Hinduism were attracting more followers than others, with an emphasis on Shaivism in the more inaccessible regions of Central India, where the dark Gods had survived in the villages through the ages and through the adoption by the ruling dynasties of the Shaiva cult in mediaeval India. Many temples came to be built which account for the splendid onrush of vital forms from Mathura and Gujrat to Ossia and Kiradu in Rajasthan to Udaipur in Malwa, at Khajuraho in Bundelkhand down to Bhubaneswar and Puri in Orissa.

The domination of the energy God Shiva seems to have been growing through the early mediaeval period in Maharashtra, Andhra and further south. The worship of this powerful God tended to be secret, because it became associated with yoga as magic and the various intricate superstitions of the people who never seem to have accepted the classical order and the exalted abstractions of any of the main religions.

Sjt. Promodchandra has recently drawn attention to some of the Shaiva cults which obsessed the imaginations of the mediaeval period.

Two of these, the *Kaula* and the *Kapalika* cults, were being actually practised around Khajuraho because there are references in the play entitled "Prabodha Chandordaya" performed in the presence of the King of the Chandela dynasty Kirtiverman at the behest of this Monarch's General Gopala about 1065 A.D. There are other references in the works of mediaeval writers, Somadeva, Kshemendra, Yamuhacharya and Ramanuja to the fascinating sensuality of Shaivism as it found expression specially in the *Kaula* and *Kapalika* cults.

As has already been indicated, these cults were rooted in the consciousness of the village peoples since the earlier periods.

The *Kaula* cult appears, however, to have been rationalised by Matsyendranatha (who lived somewhere in the 10th century) and who founded the doctrine of *Yogini Kaula*.

The ritual of the *Kaula* cult seems to have been based on a profound philosophical hypothesis. *Kaula* is the ultimate aim of the worshipper. It is the state in which the mind and sight are united and the sense organs lose their individuality. *Sakti* becomes identical with *Deva* and the sight merged into the object of visualized *Kaula* is *Sakti*. Its opposite is *Akula* which is Shiva. The unity of these two results is *Inkaula*. The ritual by which this union is established is *Kolamarga*. The conception of Shiva as *Mahalinga* is allied to the *Kaula* doctrine. The energy of *Mahalinga* is described as *Bindu* and it is characterised by *Kamakala*. The source of attraction between the male and the female and the reservoir of eternal life. The *linga* is a supreme concept and through devotion to which the knowledge of God as the author of the Universe becomes possible and deliverance attained. The ritualistic practices and meditational techniques are emphasised as the means by which magical powers are attained through yoga, disease can be conquered, energy to associate with *Yoginis* enhanced. In fact, eternal youth and immortality can be gained by partaking of the ambrosia which trickles down from the topmost lotus situated in the *Brahma Randhara*.

Like all phallic cults of the world, but rather more intensely than most, these Shaivates emphasised the symbolic nature of their rights. *Kaulamarga* is the path of controlled enjoyment of sense objects because *Yoga* and *Bhoga* are one. The process of growth through the various stages of worship is intricate, prolonged and difficult. The easiest part of it seems to have been the tasting of *Panchamrita* or *Panchmakaras*. Flowers, perfumes, flesh, fish and sweet meats were common objects used in ceremonials. *Vesya-Kumarikas* (virgin courtesans) were enjoined.

The emphasis on the exalted symbolic significance of this ritual seems to have been part of the idealistic wish fulfilment of doctrinaire theologians, seeking to adumbrate the aura of dignity and formalism around the primitive but potent magical and sensual ceremonies of a mass inured to hidden and esoteric beliefs. As the doctrine of attachment preached in the *Bhagavad Gita* remained an unattainable ideal, though it was universally preached and acclaimed, so the moral precepts which clothed psychological needs were like desire images qualified by rationalist explanations.

The actual imaginative writing of the mediaeval period presents many pictures of a lovely sensuality which, of course, the enemies of the *Kaulas* attacked mercilessly but which are not without the charm that all descriptions of the real rich life of the period display. For instance, Kshemendra recreates, with a certain lascivious hunger, the scenes of *Kaula* indulgences which show that the Hindus had a dual sense of life, on the one hand evidence of the emotional reponse to the ways of pleasure, including the play function of sex, and the metaphysical sense, eager to compromise and correlate the waves of bliss, the excitement of each nerve and tendon in the human body with the tension of each moment and the exacting discipline of thought. The so called vulgarity which later Hindus have come to see in the eroticism implicit in the *Kaula* cult is probably derived from the western Christian approach which considers the very central Hindu doctrine of the procreation of the Universe through the union of male and female as sin. In this context it is important to see that in the books of the ancient and mediaeval Hindu writers, woman does not appear as she does in European literature of that time, in the role of a mere landscape which is adorned and loved, but as the essential partner of the ritual of life. Her generative faculties are accepted as primary human facts and not open to the insinuations, ridicule and obscene jokes of those who despise sex. The concept of the sons of Gods was, for instance, admitted as an ordinary principle among the Hindus in the same way in which the Greeks practised it. The kings and noblemen whose physical defects made the birth of heirs to the throne impossible, did not feel any derogation of their authority in inviting a priest to officiate in the ceremonies through which sons could be ensured; for, after all, the maintenance of the race was a higher ideal than mere pleasure, important as the latter seems to have been to the *Nagariks* (gentlemen) and *Nagarikas* (gentlewomen) of those times.

Of course, the very idea of the wife of the householder who sought sons of God by cohabiting with a *Sarva Guru* could lend itself to caricature as in the 8th *Upadesa* of *Desopadesa*. And the orgiastic ceremony described in *Narmala*, where a *Kaula Guru* sublimates the wife of a rich nobleman disciple, seems in cold print, and subsequent colder thought, like the most debased ritual.

None of these scenes could, however, have got on to the walls of Khajuraho temples without universal acceptance of initiation ceremonies of young Hindu brides as part of the ritual of marriage, of the acceptance of union between the male and the female as the height of spiritual sensitiveness and of the extension of the pleasure of the body as the vehicle of the soul in the warm, lush universe, where people came to drink the amrit of energy from the temple and to contemplate the fundamental law of the Universe, as the mating of *Lingam* and *Yoni*.

A *Kapalika* cult, which was less rational and more instinctive, flourished at the same time as the Kaula. The *Kapalikas* were also known as *Mahavratins, Mahabhairavanusasana Parameshvarasiddhantin* and *Somasiddhantin*. The lack of a well thought out rationalisation for their practices seems to have been due to the extreme forms of secrecy in which the followers of

34

the sect indulged. For instance, they associated human sacrifice with their ritual and laid greater emphasis on the erotic impulse. Almost as ancient as the *Kaula* sect, it seems to have been feared by the people and probably evolved as a much despised secret esoteric cult, restricted to a fanatical order of the practitioners. Some light is thrown on their essential beliefs in Bhavabhuti's play *Malatimadhava*. The *Kapalikas* lived in close association with their female *yoginis* and the oldest temple of Khajuraho, the *Chausath Yogini*, is so called because it is dedicated to the 64 *yoginis*. The *Agamapramanya* of Yamunacharya (A.D. 1051) mentions that the *Kapalikas* wear the sacred thread on their ash smeared bodies, crest jewel, ornaments for ear and neck, and bear a human skull in one hand, with a club in the other. The *Kapalikas* locate the seat of the Self in the *Yoni* and by meditation on this, deliverance is achieved. According to the evidence of the play *Prabhodha Chandrodaya* mentioned above as having been performed before the Chandela King, Kirtiverman, the *Kapalikas* were known as *Soma-siddhantins* and that they believed in *Moskha* through the complete enjoyment of woman, the ideal being to become incarnate in a form like that of Shiva and enjoy the pleasures of love with a consort as beautiful as Parvati. In Rajashekhara's *Karpuramanjari*, the Kapalika Bhai-ravananda is described as heeding no *Mantras* or *Yantras* or prayers of meditation or wisdom but only wine and women through whose enjoyment he can attain deliverance.

A further concession to mankind was on the way in the philosophy called the *Tantra*, which is an affirmative creed in which the phenomenal world or *Maya*, still rejected in early mediaeval thought, is not to be rejected but embraced. As a matter of fact, Shankara, whose commentaries had brought about the earlier concession through his doctrine of *Brahman*, as pure consciousness reflected in consciousness in the illusory *Maya* world of experience, had himself sung in certain hymns and rhapsodies called *Vedanta Gitas* with a fervour that implied the possibility of release from the phenomenal ego through the recitation, memorising and meditation of the exalted utterances of god-intoxicated poetry. Thus though emphasising the ineffable transcendency of *Brahman*, the "Aum" without a second, in his philosophical writings he sings to the "second", to Maya, Mother of the world, with a passionate devotion:

Thou who bearest the manifold world of
   the visible and the invisible,
Who holdest the universe in thy womb,
Who severest the thread of the play we play
   upon this earth!
Who lightest the lamp of wisdom; who
   bringest Joy to the heart of Thy Lord, Siva!
O Thou, Queen Empress of Holy Benares!
   Divine Bestower of Food Inexhaustible,
Be gracious unto me and grant me alms.

Hymn to Annapurna

This strain of acceptance led to the popular concept that all beings are members of a single holy family, proceeding from the Aum, the only divine substance, and that realisation of God can take place by a bold affirmation of all that may ever come to be, the gods being addressed as dwelling within the microcosm.

The seeker does not, therefore, circumvent the life of sensation or emotion by crushing them within himself or shut his eyes to their manifestation, but goes through the fires of passion. The pleasure of human love is, for instance, the bliss of the Goddess in her world-creation-dance, the Joy of the urge for union of *Siva* and his *Sakti* is the inferior mode of his ego-consciousness. The passionate hero has only to wash away his sense of ego, and then the same act, which was formerly a hindrance, becomes the tide that bears him to the realisation of *Ananda*. And the same tide washes away the ego-consciousness.

As Sir John Woodroffe, the Tantric scholar, puts it succinctly: "The *Sadhaka* (the student) is taught not to think that we are one with the Divine in Liberation only, but here and now, in every act we do. For in truth all soul is *Sakti*. It is *Siva* who as *Sakti* is acting through the *Sadhaka*. When this is realised in every natural function then, each exercise thereof ceases to be a mere animal act and becomes a religious rite—a *yajna*. Every function is a part of the Divine Action (*Sakti*) in Nature. Thus when taking drink in the form of wine, the hero knows it to be *Tara Draomayi*, that is, 'The Saviour Herself in liquid form'. How, it is said, can he who truly sees in it the Saviour Mother receive from it harm? When the *Vira* eats, drinks or has sexual intercourse, he does so not with the thought of himself as a separate individual satisfying his own limited wants, an animal filching as it were from nature the enjoyment he has, but thinking of himself in such enjoyment as *Siva*, saying '*Sivoham, Bhairavoham*' (I am *Siva*).''

Sex, then, according to the *Tantra Shastras*, came to play an important symbolic role. The five good things which are only snares and dangers for the common herd, become the vehicles of liberation for the hero. Says *Siva* to *Sakti* in the *Mahanirvana Tantra:* "The five essential elements have been prescribed to be wine, meat, fish, parched grain, and the union of man with woman. The worship of Sakti without these five elements is but the practice of evil magic *abhicara*, a ritual that injures and destroys; the power that is the object of the discipline is never attained thereby, and obstacles are encountered at every step. As seed sown on barren rocks does not germinate, so worship without these five elements is fruitless.''

The Tantric *Sadhaka*, then, eats the "forbidden" fruits and, by plunging directly into the phenomena, experiences the essential non-existence of duality, realising the intrinsic purity and innocence of the seemingly dark and dangerous sphere.

He recognises the one *Sakti* in everything, the support of the world, the source of all microcosms and macrocosms, the mother of gods and spirits, the eternal beloved. And thus comes release from *Maya*, release through full enjoyment rather than rejection.

The hero must, however, make love not with hysterical reactions, but with a calm equanimity, for cohabitation *(maithuna)* is not possible in the usual animal human way of desiring, fearing and enjoying but when the hero knows himself to be identical with *Siva*.

For this purpose certain sexo-yogic practices were evolved by the Tantrics through which the human body which contains the two elements (*Siva*, primordial male or the static aspect, and *Sakti*, the primordial female or the dynamic aspect) could unite into the non-dual state of Absolute Reality. *Siva* was conceived as residing in *Sarasrara*, the cerebrum region in the head and Sakti in the *Muladhara chakra* at the bottom. Or, the right side of the body is conceived of as male and the left as female. The *Sadhaka* is enjoined to control the vital winds *apana* and *prana* associated with the two nerves, *Pingala* on the right and *Ida* on the left, and making them flow together through the middle nerve, *Sushumna. Maithuna* could also be achieved through various sexual forms of *Hatha Yoga*.

The ritual of the worship through *Panachatantra* has been described in the various *Tantras* in great detail. The most important form is Charapuja or circle worship. This rite is said to be performed in secrecy, either in an inner sanctum of a temple or in a rich Sakta household at night. A circle of a prescribed radius is drawn in the room. In the centre of the circle is drawn a *yantra* and there sits the host and his *Sakti*. The *Sakta* guests sit around with their *Saktis* beside them.

The *Saktis* can be of three different kinds: *Svivia*, or one's own wife; *Parakiva*, or another man's wife; and *Sudharni*, or common woman. Some Tantric texts maintain the *maithuna* is only possible with one's own wife while others allow the union with any women as every woman is really the embodiment symbol of *Sakti*.

A large jar is placed before the worshippers on a jewelled altar enclosed in a mystic drawing and is filled with wine. Prayers are then said to turn the wine into nectar and to obviate the curse of the sage Sukra, who had once cursed all liquor and preached prohibition.

After this, cooked meat, fish and gram are brought and consecrated by incantations and appropriate mystic gestures.

Now drinking starts and the devotees eat meat with the first cup, fish with the second and gram with the third. And afterwards the worshipper eats anything he desires.

No more than five cups of wine were allowed, the rule being: They may drink until the state of their mind is not affected. To drink beyond this is bestial. How is it possible for a sinner who becomes a fool through drinking and who maligns the *Sadhaka* of *Sakti* to say, 'I worship the *Adya Kalika* ''?

These Tantric rites were called *Kaula* rites because of their supposed *Kaula* or noble nature. And one of the main aims of these rites was to raise the devotee above all sense of right and wrong. Of course, it is very possible that the injunctions to maintain the ceremony at an exalted level show that it could degenerate into excessive drinking and hysterical *maithuna*.

The philosophical basis of the cult has been explained by Arthur Avalon in a manner which brings out its mystic meaning: "By the poison which kills all animals, by that same poison the physician destroys disease. The root of Homeopathy is to cure illness by that which causes illness. Amongst us also there is the tradition that poison is destroyed by poison. What then is that which makes man sin and die before his time, the object of contempt of all. The first amongst these causes are wine and women; meat, fish, corn are accessories. These five *tatvas* are the primary causes of the terrible incurable disease which is *Samsara* (worldly life). Man under the influence of wine becomes devoid of manliness and worthless. The stupefying power of wine and woman is so great as to attract even the pious and wise and hurl them into the abyss of darkness and ignorance. Here Shiva (the propounder of the Tantric system) prescribes poison which eradicates poison. We know as other *Sadhakas* do that this homeopathic system of Shiva is infallible and yields speedy results. He who thirsts for wine or lusts after women can be cured by this treatment within a very short time. But the physician, that is the Guru, must be experienced and skilful. A slight error in the administration of the poison may lead to fatal results. On this account Shiva said that the path of *Kaula* rite is more difficult than it is to walk on the edge of a sword or to embrace the neck of a tiger. Here we give a popular or esoteric explanation of the *Tatva*. But if the esoteric meaning of them be also known then it will be seen that in the matter of *Sadhana* they are absolutely necessary. No one who is not a *Tatva Jnani* (knower of first principles) can master their esoteric meaning.

On this account Shiva has prohibited the disclosure of the *Sadhana* to ordinary people. We have ourselves seen people who claim to be *Kaulas*, but in fact they are no better than drunkards and libertines. O Reader, blame not *Kulachara* on seeing these erring men. A libertine and drunkard can never be a *Kaula*. The *Kaula* method is unique. He cannot be a drunkard and libertine. On seeing a woman he sees his mother and *Ishtadevata* in her and in either mind or body makes obeisance to her. The Saints Gavrange, Nityananda and Advaita are brilliant examples of the true *Kaula*. In the *Mahabaratta* and *Vishnupurana* it has been said that desire cannot be quenched by the enjoyment of objects of that desire. On the contrary, desire flames up like fire when ghee is thrown upon it. This is very true. No one says that the drinking of poison will not kill. But the physician administers poison in such a

40

wonderful way that it does not kill the patient but on the contrary the poison in the body is destroyed. The way in which the Guru administers the poison of wine and thus destroys the poison of *Samsara* cannot be disclosed before the lay public and so this is prohibited by Shiva.

X

SINCE THE BUDDHA'S DECLARATION OF THE "FOUR NOBLE TRUTHS" AND the "eight-fold path" this doctrine had also gone through developments from the original negative *Hinayana* to the more positive *Mahayana*. The first struggle against Hinduism and the later influence of the subtle Hindu psychology of ritualistic worship was, among other things, the main factor in bringing about this transformation. And in the thousand years that

41

elapsed between the "enlightenment" and the beginning of the mediaeval period, much elaboration took place that tended to obfuscate the first principles and to introduce magical elements, which made this religion more amenable to the laity and also brought it into line with basic Hindu thought, until we see the emergence of Tantric Buddhism, even as we have seen the concessional doctrines of the Hindu *Tantras*.

The *Mahayana* Buddhism had interpreted the riddle of the universe through the concept of the *Bodhisattva-Avalokitesvara*.

Avalokitesvara refused *Nirvana*, because he was filled with *Karuna* "compassion". This compassion is thus the essence of the Bodhisattva and ensures his right perception of the void; and through compassion he assumes the various forms in which he appears as the saviour of beings in the phenomenal world. For instance, he becomes Vishnu for those who worship Vishnu, and Siva for those who are devoted to Siva. And, by virtue of his compassion, the Buddhas are born in this world. The quality of compassion is present in all creatures and this makes them eligible to Bodhisattvahood, for all things are of *sunyali*, the void, and the pure reflection of this void is compassion. *Karuna* holds things in manifestation, even as it withholds the Bodhisattva from *Nirvana*. The universe is compassion, which is also known as *Sunyali*, the void.

As in the Buddha's teaching, ignorance *(avidya)* is still in the *Mahayana* doctrine the cause of all suffering, the cause of bondage to the cycle of birth, rebirth, old age and death; it is still the thing which brings affliction to those who live in desire, fear, hope, despair, disgust and sorrow. But he who is cleansed and whose soul has become one with the void, is capable of a joyous wonder. Actually, those who, in their ignorance, feel themselves engulfed in pain are themselves non-beings, void and unchanging, but their ignorance makes them feel that they are in pain. The Bodhisattva is, however, capable of great delight, because where others find pain, poverty, disaster, vice or horror, pleasure, virtues, the "highest knowledge" reveals the void, the nameless, absolute, unchanging, stainless, without beginning and without end. "By those identical actions by which mortals rot in hell for hundreds of scores of cycles, the Yogi is liberated." Thus forbidden foods such as meat, fish, spicy dishes, wine and sexual intercourse are acceptable to the aspirant. Of course, they are not to be enjoyed in sensual eagerness or boredom, but to be undertaken without egoism and under the advice of a spiritual teacher, as there are difficulties and dangers attending these important indispensable practices.

The sex act affords a profound experience of the metaphysical mystery of the non-dual entity which has been made manifest as two. The coming together of the male and the female principles, and their delight, evidence their intrinsic unity and metaphysical identy. For through the sexual act, the creatures of the outside world come into touch with the metaphysical sphere of the non-dual source. Of course, the latter is not apart. In fact, it is their own essence which they experience in every impulse of compassion. Only in the sex act, the supreme realisation of compassion takes place at its supremest height, the great delight.

From the right perception of *sunyali* (the void) comes *bija* (the seed). From *bija* the conception of an icon is developed, and from that conception is derived the external representation of the icon. And through the contemplation of the icon, one's mind is united with

42

the "seed". And through this seed one returns to the void. The image may be of wood, or stone or metal, or a living model, the teacher or the devotee himself in the *Yab-Yum*, male-female embrace.

The devotee can read the *Yab-Yum* image in two ways: He can meditate on the female part as the *Sakti* or dynamic aspect of eternity, and the male as the dormant but activised element; or, the male can be regarded as the principle of the path, the way, *Upaya*, and the female, *prajna*, with which it merges, as the transcendent goal, who becomes the source in which the dynamic of enlightenment is complete, permanent brightness. Again, the dual symbol of the united couple is to be read in two ways: either the male or the female representing truth, so that the two aspects of reality are equal in status, and there is no difference between *samsara* and *nirvana* in dignity or in substance. "Suchness" is thus seen, for differences become non-existent in true enlightenment.

The Yogic practices through which the physical union of *upaya* and *prajna* are achieved are somewhat similar both in Hinduism and Mahayana Buddhism.

The origin and development of the Tantric practices are sometimes ascribed to a certain Indrabhati, King of Uddiyana, who lived in the seventh or eighth century A.D., possibly in Orissa. This Raja is the author of the *Jnansiddhi*, a treatise which describes the *Yab-Yum* initiation. And it is said that Indrabhati's daughter, Laksminkara Devi, was one of the pioneers of this aristocratic cult of love.

Certainly, some of the Tibetan images which symbolise this doctrine of the merging of opposite principles in timeless union in the transcendent one Reality are the most striking examples of the world's art.

XI

ACTUALLY, AS HAS BEEN INDICATED THROUGHOUT THESE NOTES, THERE is no room for apologies or making pretences here. The whole of the self-conscious series of erotic carvings of Indian art must be taken for what they are, the expression of the urges of its peoples, and judged internally according to the consistencies or inconsistencies in the concepts behind it, and in the light of the greater or lesser skill displayed than through aesthetic principles which are not only alien to it but are moreover reinforced by a morality totally outside the consciousness of the original builders. It is true that only a very few people can nowadays emulate the example of the great Shankara who, on visiting a legendary sage, saw him with one leg in the fire and the other in the lap of a lovely woman, and accepted the phenomenon as a matter of course. But is it likely that we can recover some part of the humility which can at least ask questions before offering summary judgements based on our own egoistic perversities? For to go to Khajuraho, Bhuvaneshwar, Konarak or Puri involves an act of surrender to the accent of other ages than our own individualist, hybrid, modern era, and the acceptance of the primary truth stated by the dramatic critic Dhananjaya, that "those who lack imagination are no better than furniture, walls or stones".

And if the miracle should happen that one's mind is transformed by the will to understand, and a certain rhythm of pride swirls down one's body at witnessing the achievement of other men, of other times, then it may be possible, after the first thrill of wonder, to allow one's curiosity to lead one from the solid plinth and the noble gateways to vaulting heights of intention and ambition behind each architrave. And one would walk around the pillars in reverence at the sheer grandeur of the execution of concepts seldom rendered in stone with quite such devotion, resulting in beauties which even in our own arbitrary sense of that word, are commensurate with some of the greatest in world art. And, then, if one's eyes, filled with the bewildering multiplicity of forms, still remain calm, there may come to be, under the immobile rim of the lashes, the promise of a spiritual insight which may penetrate beyond the flowers and the incense, and the dim oil lamps, to the dreams of these who stood poised, for certain moments, between the shining surface of reality and the inner core of the radiance, imploring with whispered chants, for the light to bend towards their heads.

KHAJURAHO

4

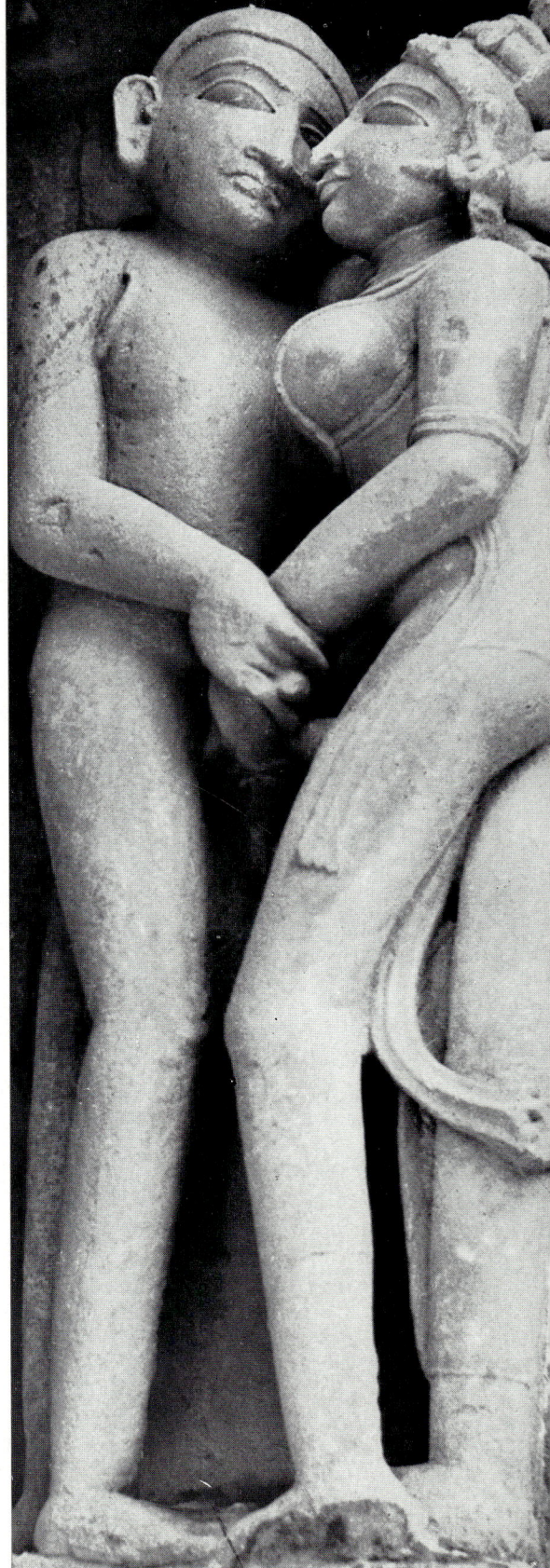

XI   XII   XIII

15

XIX

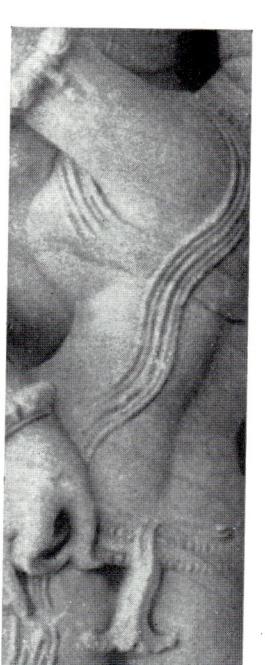

XXI-XXII

XXIII

XXIV

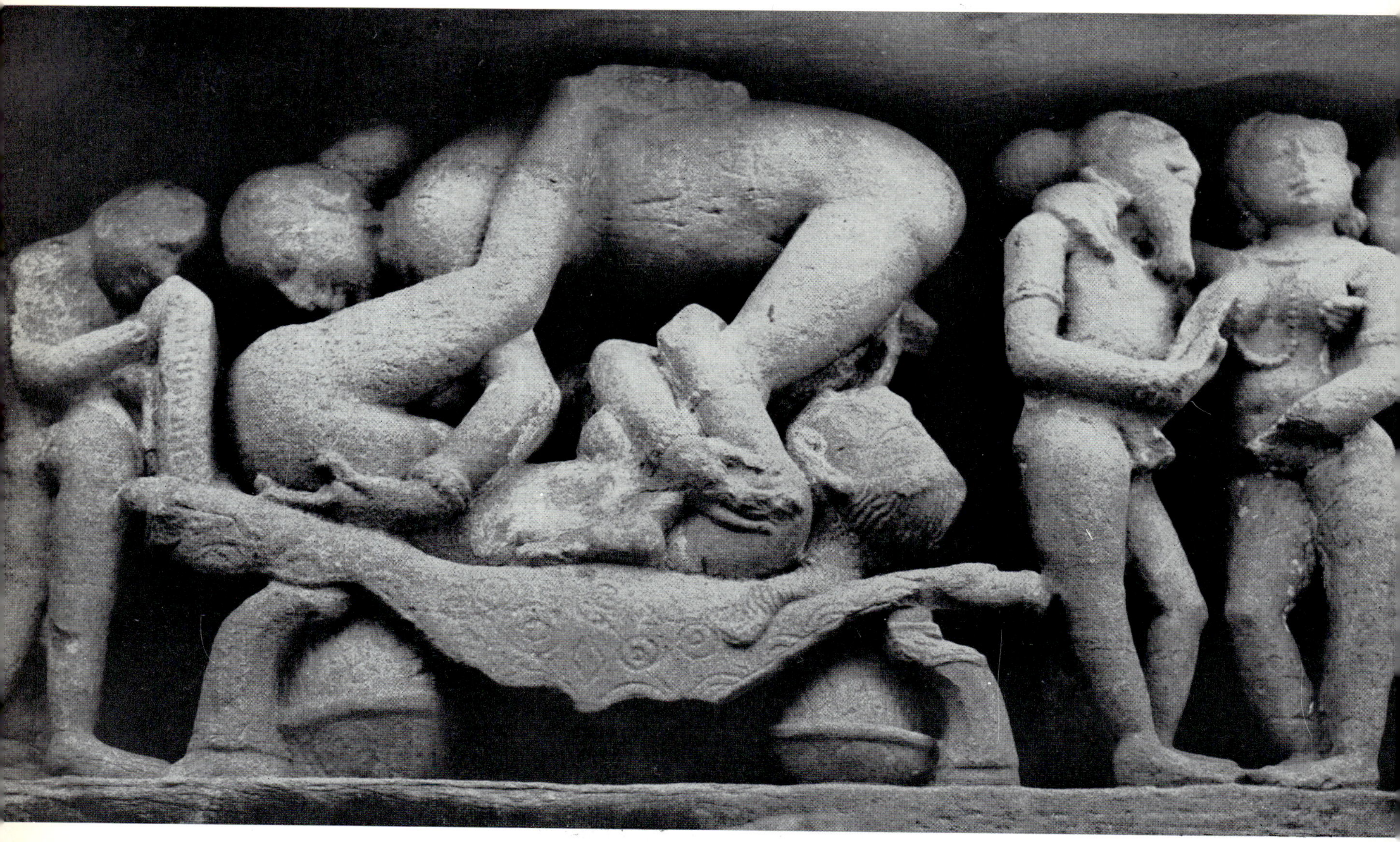

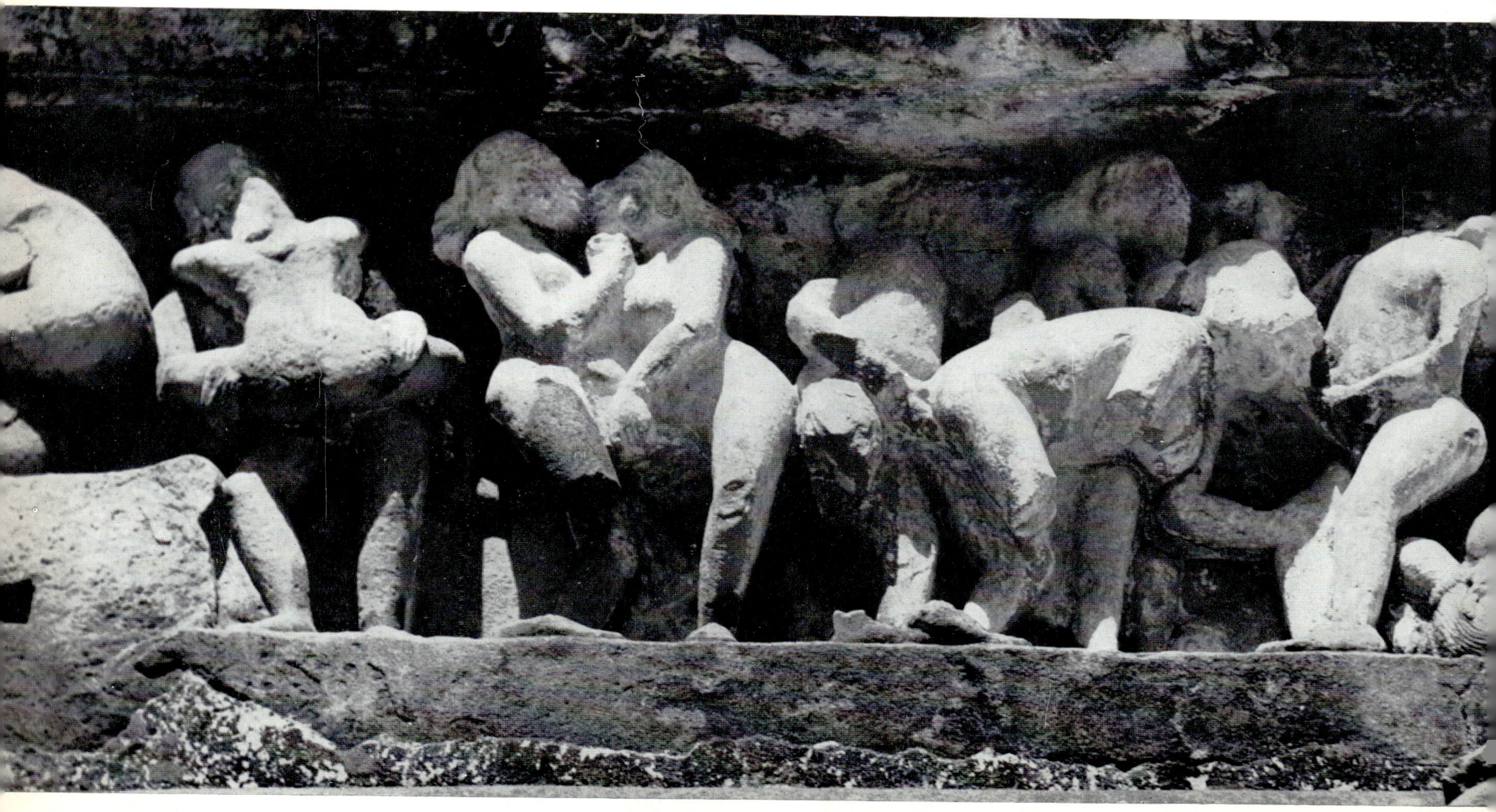

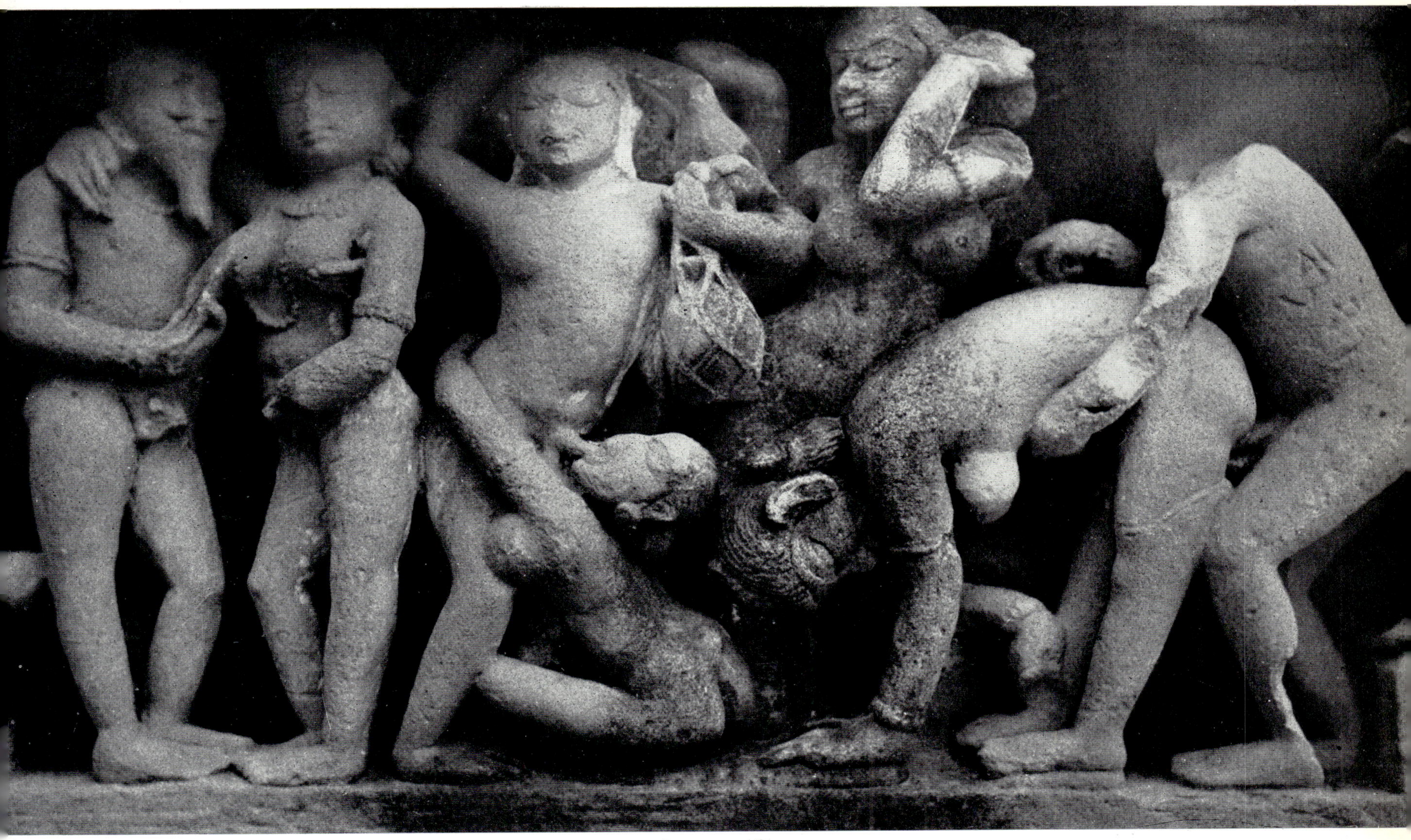

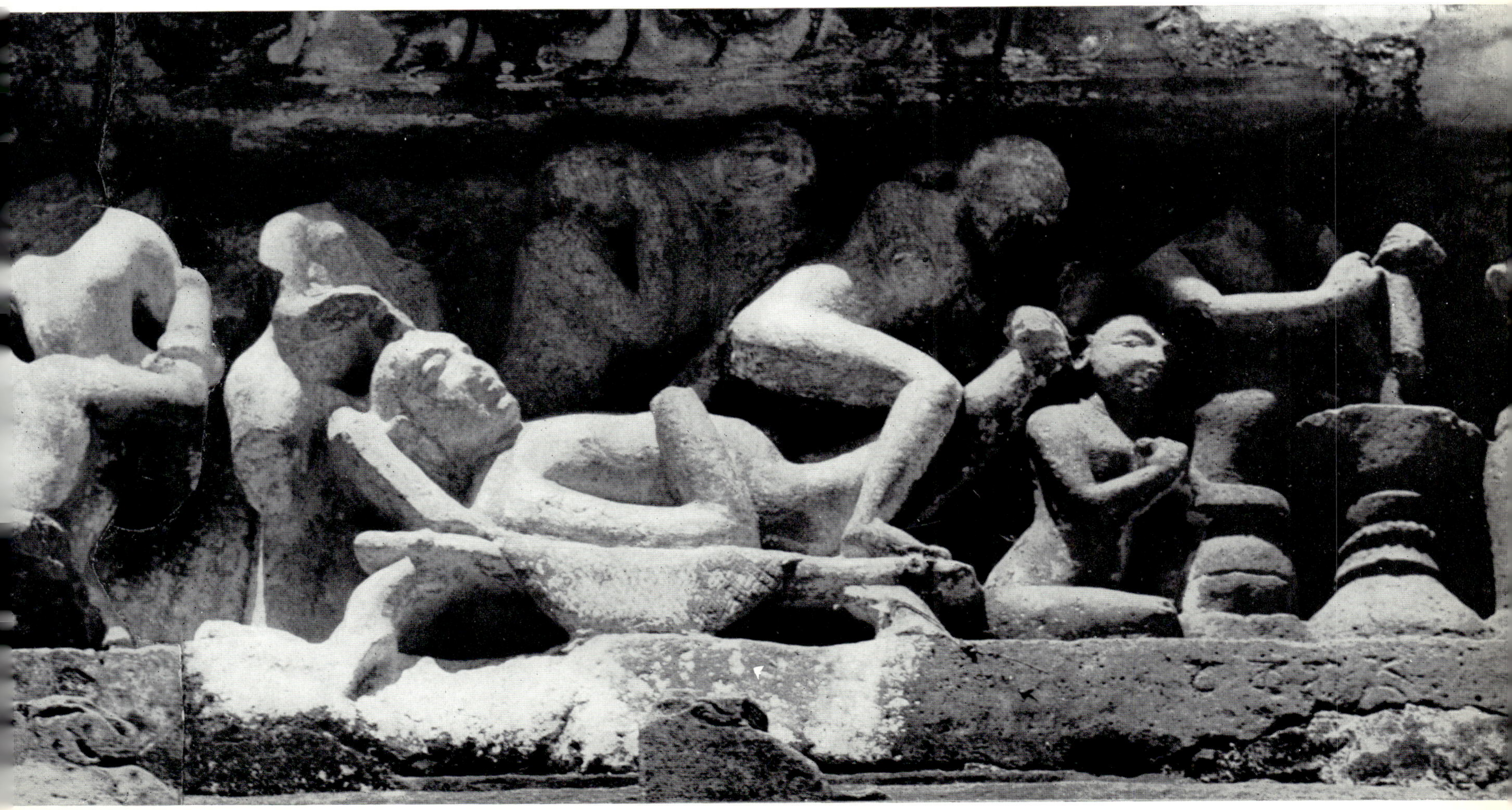

KONARAK

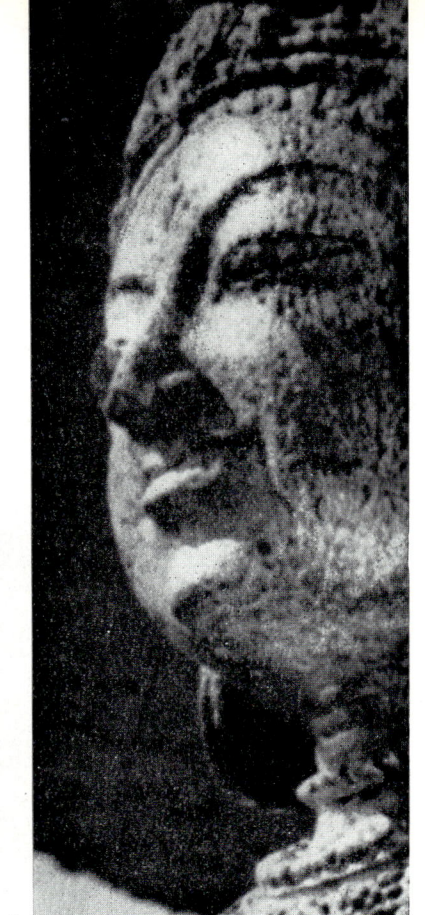

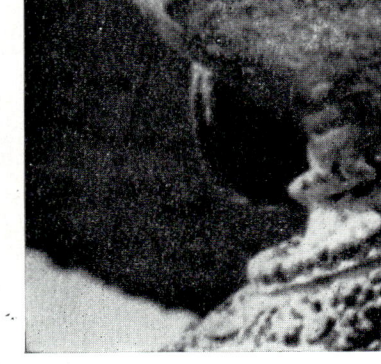

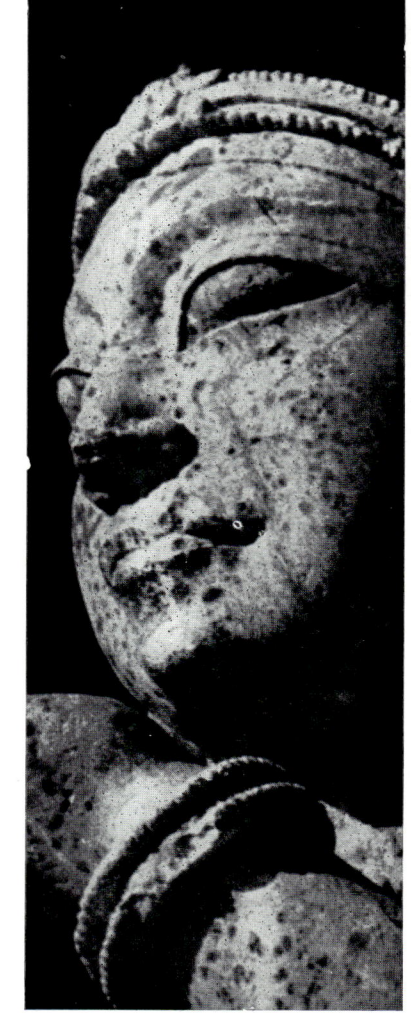

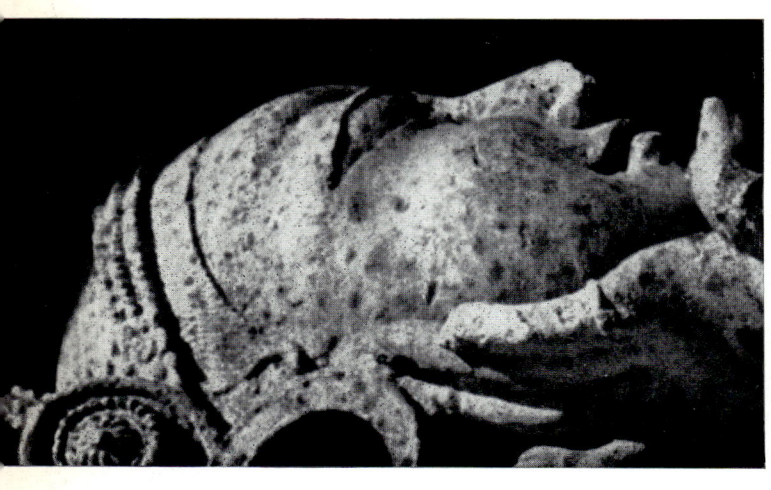

ILLUSTRATIONS

The text and illustrations of this volume
were printed on the presses of

NAGEL PUBLISHERS

in Geneva
Finished in June nineteen hundred and sixty-two

The photographs in this volume were taken by
Raymond Burnier   Moti Ram Jain
Sunil Janah   D.H. Sahiar

Plates engraved by
Clichés Richter S.A., Geneva (black and white)
and Busag AG, Bern (colour)
Binding by Nagel Publishers, Geneva

Printed in Switzerland